The *SUPERPOWER* Field Guide

EELS

BY RACHEL POLIQUIN

ILLUSTRATED BY
NICHOLAS JOHN FRITH

HOUGHTON MIFFLIN HARCOURT
Boston   New York

For Amy Tompkins and Kate O'Sullivan, with
enormous gratitude. You set me on my way. —R.P.

To Kate & Whitney, for setting me loose to run
wild with beavers . . . And, to Rachel, for her
wonderful writing in the first place. —N.J.F.

Special thanks to Ruby Banwait and the
Vancouver Aquarium.

Text copyright © 2020 by Rachel Poliquin
Illustrations copyright © 2020 by Nicholas John Frith

hmhbooks.com

The illustrations in this book were produced using a mixture of
black ink, pencil, and wax crayon on paper, in a technique known
as "preseparation." For printing purposes here, the artwork
was colored digitally.

The text type was set in Adobe Caslon Pro.
The display type was set in Sign Painter House Showcard.

Library of Congress Cataloging-in-Publication Data
Names: Poliquin, Rachel, 1975– author. | Frith, Nicholas John, illustrator.
Title: Eels : the superpower field guide / by Rachel Poliquin ; illustrated by
Nicholas John Frith. Description: Boston : Houghton Mifflin Harcourt, [2020] |
Series: Superpower field guide | Audience: Age 7–10. | Audience: Grade 4 to 6. |
Includes bibliographical references. Identifiers: LCCN 2019020309|
ISBN 9780544949218 (hardcover picture book) | ISBN 9780358272588 (trade paper)
Subjects: LCSH: Eels—Juvenile literature.
Classification: LCC QL637.9.A5 P65 2020 | DDC 597/.43—dc23
LC record available at https://lccn.loc.gov/2019020309

Manufactured in China
SCP 10 9 8 7 6 5 4 3 2 1
4500793769

THIS IS AN EEL.

Just an ordinary eel.

But even ordinary eels are extraordinary. In fact, even ordinary eels are animal superheroes.

Did I hear you say, "But aren't eels just long, slippery, slimy fishy-things that . . . hmm . . . Is there anything more to know?"

You bet your buttons there is! Imagine this: While this eel was just a baby half as big as your pinkie finger, she swam 300 million times the length of her body. If I'm doing my math right, and if you're about four feet tall, that's the same as you traveling *all the way to the moon!*

"Impossible!" you say.

I say, "You don't know eels."

But you will.

MEET OLENKA

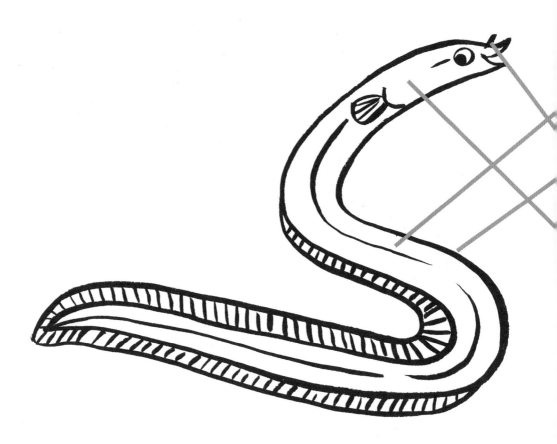

MEET OLENKA, AN ORDINARY EEL. Olenka may be plain, slimy, and the color of mud, but never, ever underestimate an eel like Olenka. Eel superpowers include:

OXYGEN SKIN

WALL CRAWLING

SLIMETASTIC SAFETY SHIELD

DOUBLE INVISIBILITY

SHAPE-SHIFTING

SUPERSECRET LAIR OF THE ABYSS
(That means a top-secret deep-sea hideout.)

GLOBE-SPANNING GRIT

OCEAN-STEALTH SUBMARINE MODE

FOUR-NOSTRILED NAVIGATION

THE MAGNETIC HEAD

So sit back and hold on tight, because Olenka is going to amaze you. I promise. In fact, Olenka's life is so unknowably extraordinary, eels have bamboozled the smartest scientists for thousands of years. You see, Olenka isn't *just* superpowered—she is also very good at keeping secrets.

Are you ready? Allow me to introduce **OLENKA, MIGRATING MISTRESS OF MYSTERY.**

THE EEL OF MYSTERY

THE FIRST THING YOU NEED TO KNOW about Olenka is that she is mysterious. *Deeply* mysterious. Of course, all animals have at least a dash of secrecy—scientists don't know everything about every creature. But Olenka and her family, the European eels, are truly, weirdly, deeply, fantastically mysterious. No doubt about it.

European eels live in European rivers and rivers throughout the British Isles, Scandinavia, parts of Russia, and North Africa. Nothing mysterious there. But *where* do baby European eels come from? Nobody *really* knows. Where do they go at the end of their lives? Ditto. Scientists can draw a big circle on a map where they think Olenka was born, and she was probably born from an egg, because that's how other eels do it. But nobody really knows for sure, because *no one has ever found a European eel egg*. Ever. Can you believe it?

People have known about eels since the beginning of time. So how can it be that no one, not even among the best scientists in the world, has ever found an eel egg? It's *very* strange. I call it **THE GREAT EEL MYSTERY.** And this is just one of Olenka's many mysteries. There are mysteries at the end of her life too, and mysteries deep inside her brain, and a very large, very bad mystery that might swallow eels into darkness forever.

But let's forget about all that for now. Let's start in the middle of the story and talk about what we *do* know about Olenka.

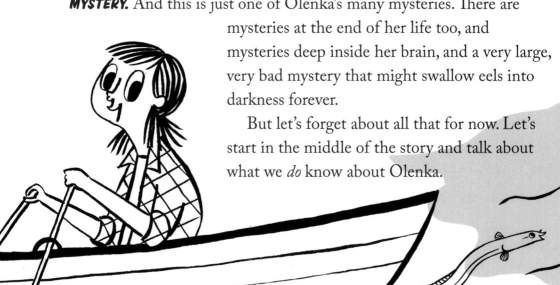

EXTRAORDINARILY ORDINARY

WHAT MAKES OLENKA ALL THE MORE MYSTERIOUS is how very ordinary she seems for most of her life.

Here she is at home in her ordinary river. It's a pretty river, north of Saint Petersburg, running through a quiet part of the Russian countryside. The river is not too fast, not too slow, with just the right amount of mud at the bottom.

Olenka is a nocturnal predator, which means she lazes her days away, curled up in her burrow at the bottom of the muddy river. Then, by moonlight, she gobbles snails, little fishes, bugs, and worms. It all seems perfectly, pleasantly ordinary, doesn't it?

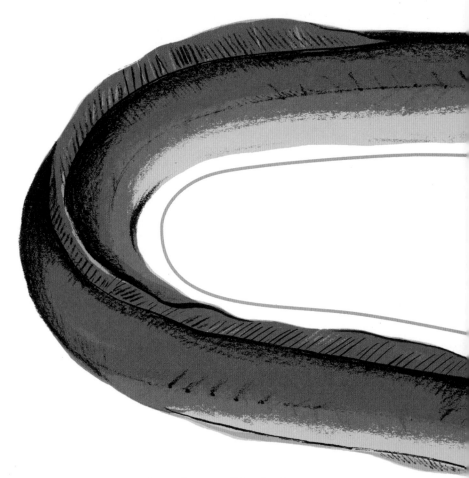

And it gets more unexcitingly ordinary. Olenka has spent *eighteen years* here without moving more than 100 yards (90 meters) in either direction. If you lived nearby, you could have visited her every day for eighteen years—every day for 6,574 days!—and found her exactly where she'd been the day before.

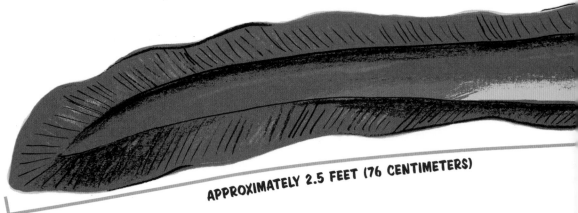

APPROXIMATELY 2.5 FEET (76 CENTIMETERS)

Her back is an ordinary fishy-brown color. Her belly is fishy yellow. She's about two and a half feet long (76 centimeters), which is not too big and not too small. In fact, everything about Olenka is perfectly, plainly, boringly ordinary.

*ACTUAL SIZE

I know what you're thinking. You're thinking I've made a mistake, that I've confused ordinary Olenka with some far more exotic eel. Like the false moray, which glows neon green under a full moon. Or the Japanese dragon moray, with its nostril horns and polka dots.

But I haven't made a mistake. Olenka may seem humdrum, drab, and boring, but don't be fooled by this quiet homebody. Soon she'll decide *it's time.* Nobody knows how or why she decides, but when she does, she'll become one of the most mysterious animals on earth. That time is coming soon, I think. While we wait, let's meet Olenka's family.

KNOW YOUR EELS

ALL TRUE EELS BELONG TO an animal order called Anguilliformes (ann-gwilly-FORM-ees). Anguilliformes is a big and important-sounding word, but it really only means "long and wiggly," or "eel-shaped" if you want to be perfectly precise. (*Anguilla* is Latin for "eels" and *formes* means "form or shape.") And it's true: all eels are eel-shaped.

The next thing you need to know is that there are around 800 species of true eels. That's a lot! They all live in the sea, except for just nineteen species of *freshwater eels* (including Olenka), which spend most of their lives in rivers and lakes. Some eels are very thin. Others are pudgy with polka dots. A few have neon nostril fans, and a couple are grumpy enough to bite off your thumb. So watch out! True eels are not ordinary fish.

> When scientists named European eels, they didn't try very hard. Olenka's scientific name is *Anguilla anguila*, which means "eel eel" or maybe "eely eel."

But they *are* fish—did you know that? True eels are honest-to-goodness fish, just like salmon or goldfish. But true eels are fish with a difference. True eels have flair! Especially Olenka. She's got some real eel gumption.

THE OLD MAN AND THE SEA

NOTABLE EELS

FRESHWATER EELS: The freshwater eels are the only eels to live their adult lives in fresh water. They include European eels, American eels, and Japanese eels.

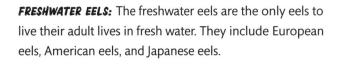

MORAY EELS: These predators have a second set of jaws inside their throats that snap forward, seize prey, and drag it down their throats.

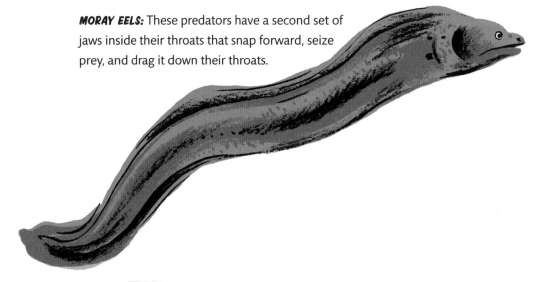

SPOTTED GARDEN EELS: Supercute and tiny, garden eels dig vertical burrows in the sea floor. They live in groups and look like an adorable garden of bobbing worms.

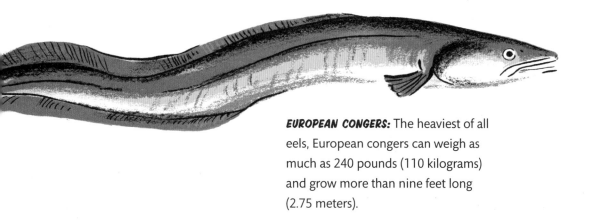

EUROPEAN CONGERS: The heaviest of all eels, European congers can weigh as much as 240 pounds (110 kilograms) and grow more than nine feet long (2.75 meters).

RIBBON EELS: With neon nostrils and bands of bright blue and neon yellow, ribbon eels are the beauties of the eel family.

GULPER EELS: These scary eels of the deep have loosely hinged mouths much larger than their bodies for swallowing fish much bigger than they are. *Yikes!*

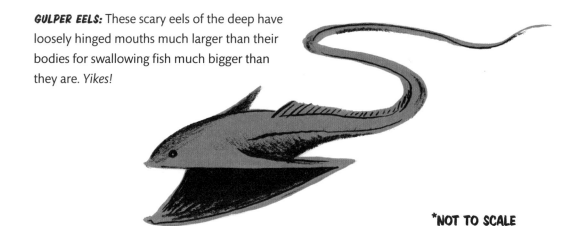

*NOT TO SCALE

Now, if you were paying attention, and I'm sure you were, you might have noticed I keep saying "true eels." That's because not everything we call an eel is actually an eel. And you need to know that one of the most famous eels in the world is a phony.

Can you guess which it is?

Answer: The electric eel—it's actually a knife fish. But don't be disappointed. Electric eels aren't *that* special. There are 500 different kinds of electric fish in the world, like electric rays, electric catfish, electric ghost fish . . . I could go on. Olenka might not be able to zap you with a biological battery, but Olenka can do things ordinary fish don't even dare dream about, which brings us to her first superpower: **OXYGEN SKIN!**

A few more impostors: Wolf eels are not true eels, nor are rubber eels, spiny eels, swamp eels, or eelpouts. Also, a lot of fish look like eels but aren't, like rope fish and pipefish. Don't be fooled by their long and wiggly shape! And let's not forget sea snakes, swimming worms, and floating sausages. None of them are true eels either.

SUPERPOWER #1

OXYGEN SKIN

I BET A LOT OF TROUT spend their days wondering if some other pond is nicer than their pond. Maybe that pond has tastier bugs, but the trout will never know. Trout don't have legs. And even if they did have legs, they don't have lungs.

You see, instead of lungs, most fish have *gills*—those are the slits that open and close on the sides of a fish's face. If you ever get the chance to look inside a fish gill, you'll see layers of pink, feathery tissues—those are the *gill filaments*.

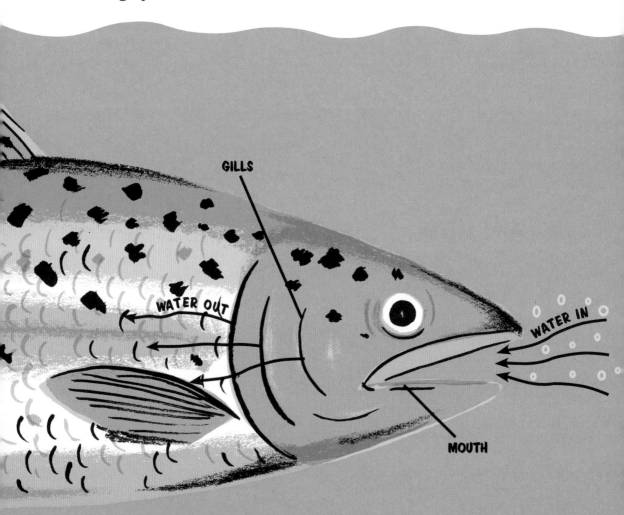

Here's a crazy fact: A few fish *do* have lungs. Guess what these fish are called? Lungfish! How unimaginative! But you'll never forget the name.

Trout breathe by slurping water into their mouths and pushing it out through their gills. As the water flows out, the gill filaments suck **oxygen** from the water and absorb it into the fish's blood. But gill filaments are too soft and floppy to work out of water, which is why trout can't live out of water.

But as I said, Olenka is a fish with real eel gumption! She isn't going to let a floppy fish gill stand in her way of greatness. If she ever thought another river was better than hers, she'd hitch up her skirt (as the expression goes; eels don't wear skirts, but you knew that), wiggle out of her river, cross the meadow, and find a better place to live.

WHAT DID I JUST SAY?

That's right . . . Olenka *can cross a meadow!* **OLENKA IS A FISH OUT OF WATER!**

But that's impossible. Everyone knows Fish Rule #1 is "All fish live in water." Right?

Wrong! Fish Rule #1 is "For every fishy rule, there is always a fishy exception." And Olenka is most definitely a fishy exception.

But how? Olenka doesn't have lungs, and her gills are actually quite small. So how does she do it?

You think she holds her breath?

It's a good guess. And, to be honest, I have no idea if she can. But I do know that European eels can survive out of water not just for a few minutes, not just for a couple of hours . . . Olenka can survive out of water for *two whole days!* And nobody, not even a superpowered eel, can hold their breath for that long. Any more guesses?

Okay. I'll tell you. Olenka can breathe through her skin! **HOLY FISHHOOKS!**

Instead of using gills or lungs, Olenka can absorb the oxygen she needs through her skin, just like frogs, salamanders, and other *amphibians*. Her skin has to be moist to trap the oxygen bubbles, which is why she prefers to travel by night—less fear of drying out. Then, tiny

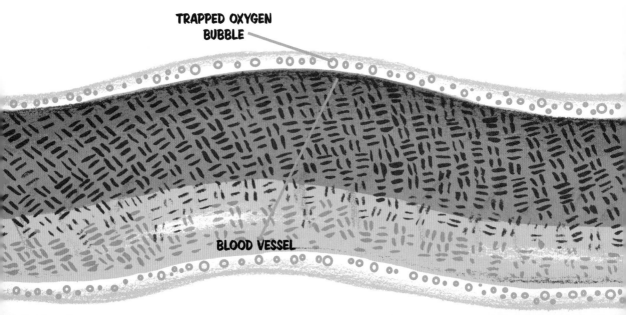

TRAPPED OXYGEN
BUBBLE

BLOOD VESSEL

blood vessels under her skin absorb the oxygen bubbles into her bloodstream. Olenka is so good at getting oxygen through her skin that even when she's in water, she gets at least half her oxygen that way, maybe even all of it.

Scientists call it *cutaneous respiration,* but I call it Incredible! Improbable! Utterly Gobsmackable! If you had **OXYGEN SKIN,** you could use your foot as a snorkel and spend hours with your head underwater!

Of course, **OXYGEN SKIN** won't do a fish any good if it can't move on land. Even if trout could breathe out of water, their fishy bodies are too round and plump to do more than flop about. But Olenka's long and skinny body can wriggle just like a snake. As long as the grass is a bit moist, Olenka can wriggle for miles! She moves forward in a wavy motion that starts at her tail and wiggles through her body to her head. To go backwards, she reverses the wave. And yes, that means eels can swim backwards.

According to French farming folklore, eels leave their rivers at night to feast on peas in the vegetable patch. But don't believe it.

A fish that can cross a meadow is impressive. But what about a fish that can climb a wall?

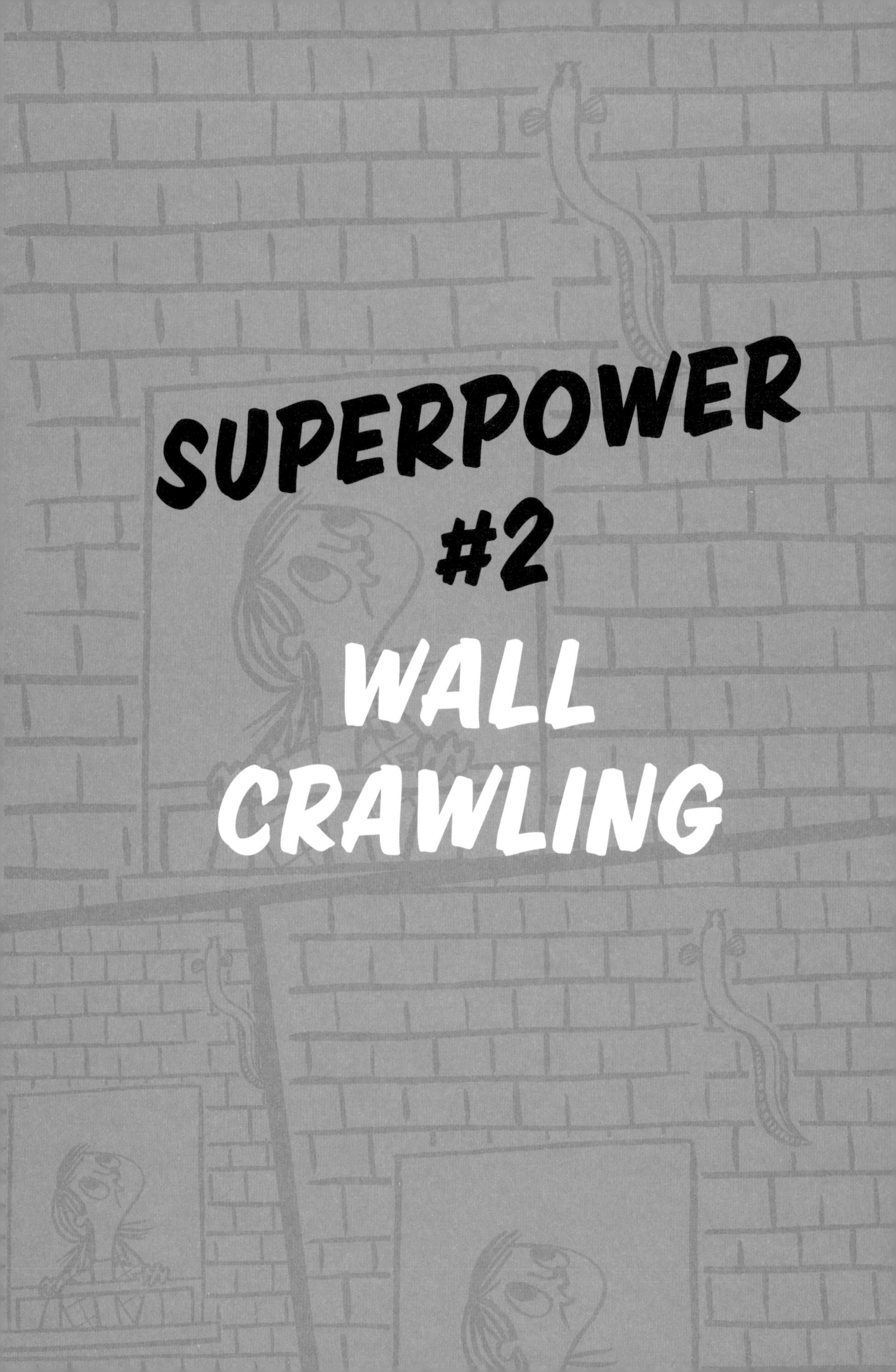

SUPERPOWER #2

WALL CRAWLING

WHEN OLENKA WAS JUST A LITTLE EEL, less than four inches (10 centimeters) long, she swam for months and months upstream in search of just the right spot in just the right river. All little eels do this. (Actually, scientists think only female eels do. But more on that later.) They begin in springtime, thousands of them altogether, each swimming in her own particular direction, always in the dark secrecy of night, always hiding in daytime. Some eels travel for hundreds of miles inland, overland, upland until they find the perfect spot to spend their adult lives.

How do little eels know which is the right spot for them? Nobody knows. But I will tell you that this strange upstream journey is your first clue in **THE GREAT EEL MYSTERY.** It means Olenka wasn't born in her river. She was born somewhere far away.

Little Olenka swam and swam upriver, and it wasn't easy. One night, she came to a stone wall blocking the river.

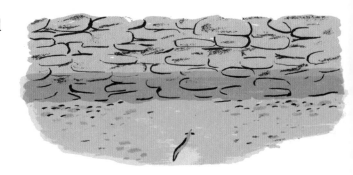

Another night it was an enormous pile of logs as tall as four grown men.

And one night she came to a towering waterfall that must have been 100 feet (30.5 meters) tall. That's as high as a 10-story building!

But did little Olenka give up? Did she settle for some other river?

Of course not! Little Olenka wriggled up the wall, over the logs, and yes, my friends, she **WALL-CRAWLED** up the rocks beside that 100-foot waterfall! As long as the obstacle is damp, a bit rough, and has cracks for daytime hiding, nothing can stop a little eel!

Spider-Man uses supersticky spider hands to climb. Olenka uses the *surface tension* of the water—that's the slightly elastic force that holds water together. Once she grows bigger than about five inches (13 centimeters), she'll lose the ability to climb. But as long as she weighs less than a pencil, or about 0.2 ounces (5 grams), the surface tension of the water will hold her to the wet wall. And because her tiny body is so long and snaky, she just wriggles on up.

OXYGEN SKIN. WALL CRAWLING. Are you thinking what I'm thinking? If so, you must be thinking that Olenka can't possibly be a fish. She must be a snake in disguise.

FISHY BUSINESS

LET'S TEST WHETHER OLENKA REALLY IS A FISH. We'll
compare her to a snake and that trout. I'll keep score.

> **GILLS:** Snakes don't have them. Trout and Olenka do.
> One point for "fish."
> **FINS:** Snakes don't have them. Trout and Olenka do.
> Another point for "fish."

But while we're talking fins, I should mention that Olenka's fins aren't anything like a trout's. As you can see, the trout has two *pectoral fins* (one on either side of its face), three fins on the bottom, two fins on the top, and a tail fin, for a grand total of eight fins.

Olenka has two pectoral fins, just like the trout, but her only other fin is a long ribbon that runs down her back, around her nubby end, and back along her underside. Scientists say her *dorsal fin* (that's the big back fin) is fused with her *caudal fin* (that's the tail fin), which is fused with her *anal fin* (that's the little fin on the trout's back-end underside). And that's how most eels do fins, although lots of eels (like morays) don't have pectoral fins, and a few eels (like some snake eels) don't have any fins at all. So maybe a half point for "snake."

> **BODY SHAPE:** Two points for "snake."

> **SCALES:** Snakes have them. So do trout. But eels don't! Well, most eels don't. Olenka and the freshwater eels do, but their scales are so strange, you can't *really* call them scales. For starters, they're indented in her skin, almost like cuts. And they aren't overlapping half-circles, like most animal scales. They're arranged in a geometric pattern like a parquet floor or a snazzy wallpaper design. So that's no points for "snake" or "fish."

SKIN: Snakes have dry skin. Fish are slippery. Olenka is *very* slippery. One point for "fish."

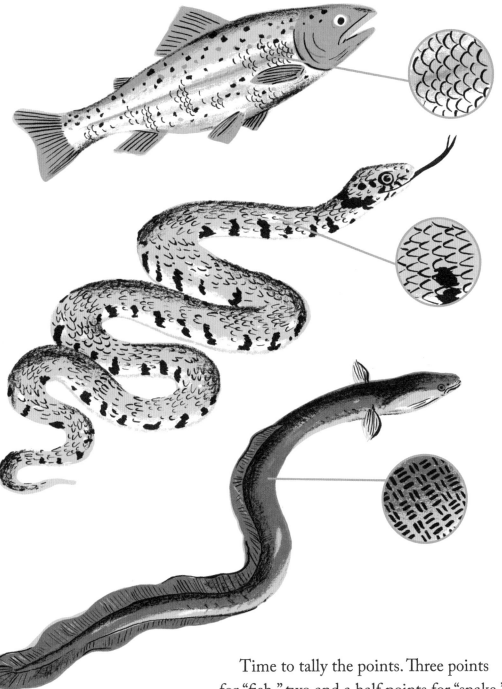

Time to tally the points. Three points for "fish," two and a half points for "snake."

"FISH" WINS!

Eels are superslimy, but they are not the slimiest fish. That honor goes to the hagfish, also known as the slime fish. When threatened, a scared hagfish oozes buckets of slime—up to five and a half gallons (20 liters) in mere seconds—that clog the attacker's gills.

You knew that already, but it's always good to double-check.

But speaking of slipperiness, do you know the expression "slippery as an eel"? It means something too slippery to hold, or impossible to catch. You probably know most fish are pretty slippery, but eels might be one of the slipperiest. Which also means they are one of the slimiest. Olenka is coated in such thick slime, she looks like she is living inside a jelly tube.

Did you just say, "Eww . . . gross"?

Yes, slime is gross. But it's also superpowered!

SUPERPOWER #3

SLIMETASTIC SAFETY SHIELD

YOU'VE PROBABLY SEEN BATMAN IN HIS BATSUIT. It's gray with black underpants, black boots, a yellow utility belt, and a cape—or it was before Batman bought his new suit. But whatever color it is, Batman's suit is always bulletproof, fireproof, and generally an indestructible safety shield for the Dark Knight.

Olenka has a super safety suit too. It's not black or yellow, and it doesn't come with underpants, but Olenka's **SLIMETASTIC SAFETY SHIELD** has more superpowers than Batman's utility belt.

FIRST: It's a shield. Scales give most fish protection. But since Olenka doesn't have ordinary scales, she has extra-thick slime. It may not be bulletproof, but thick slime protects her skin from scrapes and cuts. If a patch rubs off, it's sort of like Batman tearing a hole in his suit.

SECOND: It's a bug blaster. Slime protects Olenka from infections caused by bacteria and other nasty stuff in the water. Slime also makes it harder for *parasites* to cling to her skin.

THIRD: It makes **OXYGEN SKIN** work. Olenka's skin has to be moist in order for her to breathe. A thick layer of slime stops her skin from drying out.

FOURTH: It's aerodynamic. Slime makes Olenka super smooth and slippery for speedy getaways. It also makes eels absolutely impossible to catch by hand.

FIFTH: It's a blanket. Olenka lives in Russia. It's co-o-old in winter. When the river freezes over, Olenka buries herself in mud at the bottom and hibernates until spring. A thick layer of slime helps Olenka stay warm.

SIXTH: It's a spacesuit for traveling between worlds. You see, moving between watery worlds can kill most fishes, but Olenka has a **SLIMETASTIC SPACESUIT** for superpowered survival! This probably doesn't make any sense, but that's all I'm saying for now—it's your second clue to **THE GREAT EEL MYSTERY.**

Okay. **TIME FOR YOUR FIRST QUIZ!**

QUIZ #1

PLEASE ANSWER TRUE OR FALSE.

1. Eels were the first fish in space.

2. European eels are part snake. That's why they're the only fish that can breathe out of water.

3. Eels make excellent snorkels.

4. Eel slime makes great wallpaper glue. Better yet, paint the slime on your walls to keep them strong and straight.

5. The real reason no one has ever found an eel egg is that they don't exist. Eels are born when lightning strikes muddy water by moonlight. It's a magical mystery!

ANSWERS:

1. **FALSE.** Eels have never been to space, but other fishes have. The first fish in space were two little but very sturdy mummichogs sent up in a rocket in 1973. Scientists wanted to see how fish would handle life without gravity. They did just fine!

2. **FALSE.** Eels are 100 percent eel. Freshwater eels are the only eels that can breathe through their skin, but they are most certainly **NOT** the only fish that can breathe out of water. Snakeheads, walking catfish, climbing perch, and mudskippers can all survive out of water—mudskippers even prefer life on land. And here's a bonus fact: Electric eels are obligate air-breathers, which means electric eels **MUST** breathe air. They rise to the surface and gulp air from the world above. If they don't, they drown! A fish that drowns in water! Crazy, right?

3. **FALSE.** That's totally ridiculous. Don't ever try such a thing.

4. **TRUE.** I doubt anyone has ever used eel slime as wallpaper glue, but I bet it would work. Many eels live in burrows they've dug in the riverbed, the ocean floor, or a reef wall. The slime from their bodies helps harden the walls, a bit like cement, to prevent their burrow from collapsing.

5. **FALSE.** But it is true that eels are so mysterious, for thousands of years people believed they were born in strange ways. I think it's time to explain the mystery, don't you?

THE MYSTERY AT THE BEGINNING

TO UNDERSTAND JUST HOW MYSTERIOUS European eels really are, we need to go back in time. Way, way back. Back to some of the earliest human records, before Europe was even called Europe, and before eels were called eels, because that's how old **THE GREAT EEL MYSTERY** is. I don't know what eels were called back then, but I do know that humans living thousands of years ago knew eels. They fished for them. They ate them. They told stories about them, and drew pictures of them on cave walls. But for all those thousands of years, no one knew where eels came from.

You see, most fish are born from eggs released into the water by
female fish. Maybe you've gone fishing and caught a female salmon ready
to spawn and seen the hundreds of orangy-pink eggs inside. You might
have eaten sushi with fish eggs on top or nibbled *caviar,* which is a fancy
word for the tiny black eggs of sturgeon.

But for the thousands and thousands of years that people caught eels,
no one *ever* found an egg inside a female eel. Weirder still—no one *ever*
saw a baby eel. Since most fish eggs are about the size of peas, most
newly hatched fish are pea-size too. But the smallest eels anyone ever
found were nearly three inches (7.5 centimeters) long. Hardly babies! In
fact, scientists now think three-inch eels might already be three years old.
If you know anything about three-year-old humans, you know they can
walk and talk and eat sandwiches and draw pictures of cars and rainbows.
Three years is the entire lifespan of some fishes. What I'm trying to say
is—three years is a *really* long time! So where were the baby eels?

Many great thinkers began to think that maybe eels weren't born in the normal fishy way. Maybe they were born from strange magic. A famous ancient philosopher named Aristotle said that eels didn't have parents at all but just grew mysteriously from mud or maybe from the guts of earthworms that lived in mud. Others said eels were born when hairs from a horse's tail fell into water. Still others believed adult eels scraped their sides against rocks, and baby eels were born from their skin flakes.

They were all wrong. Eels are born in the normal fishy way, except for one tiny, important difference: *Baby eels are invisible!* Times two!

SUPERPOWER #4

DOUBLE INVISIBILITY

AS YOU PROBABLY KNOW, being invisible means that you are very hard or impossible to see. Like Invisible Woman—she can suddenly disappear, right before your eyes. But there is another kind of invisibility. I'm most definitely not invisible, but if I sit in a rowboat (also not invisible) in the middle of a vast ocean thousands of miles wide, I'd quickly become pretty darn hard to see. Unless you knew *exactly* where to look, you'd never find me.

Now, what if you put Invisible Woman in an *invisible* rowboat in the middle of that vast ocean? Do you think you could find her? Not in a million years. And that's exactly how Olenka's **DOUBLE INVISIBILITY** works. Let me explain.

Here is what Olenka looked like a few weeks after she was born. Pretty darn invisible, no? Scientists call baby fish **larvae**. But baby

OLENKA

eels have a special name, just like how baby cats are called kittens and baby dogs are puppies. A baby eel is called a **leptocephalus** (LEP-toe-SEF-a-lus), which means "slim head." And believe me, leptocephali (LEP-toe-SEF-a-lie; that's more than one) are paper-thin. They're made mostly of jelly, which is transparent and almost invisible. Their organs are tiny and almost invisible. And they don't have red blood cells, so their blood is *completely* invisible!

Baby Olenka is pretty well invisible inside this jar, and you know *exactly* where to look. But imagine trying to find her in a vast ocean. That's what I call **DOUBLE INVISIBILITY!**

Did I hear you say, "Wait a minute! I thought Olenka lived in a pleasant river just north of Saint Petersburg in Russia. What is this vast ocean you keep talking about?"

Aha! Clever you! You've just found your third clue in **THE GREAT EEL MYSTERY.** As a prize, here's your fourth clue:

Lots of baby animals look exactly like their parents but itsy-bitsy. Baby zebras, baby dogs, baby elephants—it's pretty clear what animals they'll grow into. But tadpoles don't look anything like frogs, and caterpillars don't look like butterflies. And yet, tadpoles turn into frogs, and some caterpillars become beautiful butterflies.

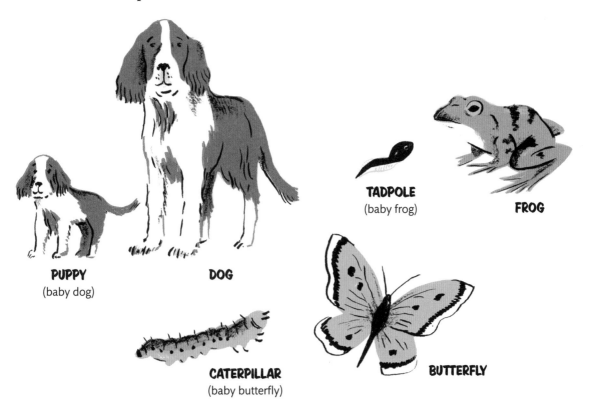

PUPPY
(baby dog)

DOG

TADPOLE
(baby frog)

FROG

CATERPILLAR
(baby butterfly)

BUTTERFLY

The big word for this process is **metamorphosis,** which means *to change completely*. And that brings me to Olenka's next extraordinary superpower: **SHAPE-SHIFTING**.

SUPERPOWER #5
SHAPE-SHIFTING

SHAPE-SHIFTING IS ONE OF THE GREATEST SUPERPOWERS of all time.

Being superstrong or superfast is impressive, but completely transforming into something else is downright amazing. Like how Bruce Banner becomes the giant green Hulk when he's angry. Or how Mystique can shape-shift to look exactly like someone else. Olenka is also a shape-shifter, and she does it again and again throughout her life.

Eighteen years ago, when Olenka swam and swam to find her river, she looked like this:

4 INCHES (10.16 CENTIMETERS)

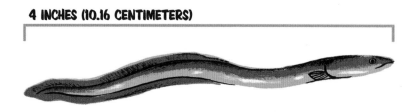

These mini eels are called **elvers**. They're pretty much what you'd expect a young eel to look like.

But a few weeks before, Olenka looked like this:

3 INCHES (7.6 CENTIMETERS)

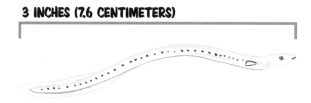

A glass noodle with two black dots for eyes! These eels are called **glass eels**.

And before that, Olenka looked like this:

3 INCHES (7.6 CENTIMETERS)

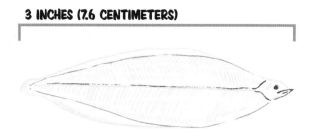

It's a leaf! It's a see-through fish! It's a leptocephalus!

*ACTUAL SIZE

Not what you were expecting, is it? It's not what anyone was expecting, which is why no one ever found a baby eel. You can't find something if you don't know what you're looking for.

In fact, way back in 1856, someone did find exactly such a see-through fish. His name was Johann Kaup, and he thought he'd discovered a new fish, never before seen by human eyes. So he named it—*Leptocephalus brevirostris,* which is a fancy scientific way of saying "slim-head short-snout." (And that's why a baby eel is still called a leptocephalus.)

So how did anyone figure out slim-head short-snouts were actually baby eels?

Well, it took a good bit of wondering by two good scientists, who just happened to be in the right place at the right time on a particularly wild and stormy day.

THE EEL AND THE SEA

IF YOU LIKE WILD TIDES AND DANGEROUS WATERS, there is a narrow bit of the Mediterranean Sea that you would love. It lies between the mainland of Italy and the island of Sicily and is famous for its churning waves and roiling whirlpools. It's called the Strait of Messina.

The tides in the strait churn so fiercely that they sometimes scoop fish from the very bottom of the sea—strange creatures even fishermen never catch—and toss them onto the beach. It was here that Kaup first found his slim-head short-snout, and it was here, half a century later, on a particularly wild day, that two scientists named Giovanni Battista Grassi and Salvatore Calandruccio found thousands of slim-head short-snouts on the beach.

These little fishes were very, very rare—only a few people had seen one, let alone thousands, and Grassi and Calandruccio were not going to waste their luck. With so many to examine, they began to wonder: Maybe these weren't adult fish like Kaup thought. Maybe they were the larvae of some already-known fish. After all, lots of fish larvae are transparent. But which fish could it be? And how to find out?

Grassi wondered if the slim-head short-snouts might have the same number of muscle sections as an adult fish had **vertebrae**. Vertebrae are the bones in our spine that run in a line from the base of our skull down our back. They're easy to see and count. Muscle sections, however, on tiny, almost-invisible fish are just tiny, almost-invisible lines. They're very, very hard to see and count. So much work! And maybe it would be pointless—maybe they weren't larvae but just weird-looking adult fish, like Kaup said.

But our two scientists couldn't help wondering. So they rolled up their sleeves, set up their microscopes, and got to work. They carefully counted tiny lines on fish after fish after fish after fish. The average number was 115.

Humans have thirty-three vertebrae. A trout can have sixty. The larvae were likely from a fish longer than a trout. Maybe an eel? But all the eels living in the Mediterranean Sea had more than 124. Guess which eel has an average of 115 vertebrae? You guessed it: the European eel.

But what was a European eel—a fish that spends its entire life in a freshwater river—doing in the Mediterranean Sea? To test their crazy theory, the scientists put a few slim-head short-snouts in a tank of salty water and waited.

Until one day . . .

GREAT MOONS OF KRYPTON—there was an eel in the tank!

Grassi and Calandruccio hadn't simply discovered what baby eels look like. They'd also discovered that freshwater eels were *born at sea!* It was a scientific breakthrough! A truly wonderful scientific discovery. No doubt about it.

However, sometimes the most wonderful scientific discoveries don't solve the mystery at all. They make the mystery bigger and deeper and stranger. Grassi and Calandruccio had explained why no one had ever found an eel egg in a river, but they had opened an even bigger can of wiggling, squirming mystery.

Have you heard the expression "caught between a rock and a hard place"? It means having only two choices, both of which are bad. Perhaps the very first rock and hard place were in the Strait of Messina. Two terrible sea monsters named Charybdis and Scylla were said to attack ships from either side as they sailed through the dangerous waters. Scylla was a rocky shoal (or a six-headed monster), while Charybdis created fearsome whirlpools to suck ships down to the bottom of the sea. I told you there were dangerous waters!

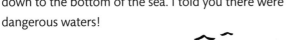

THE EVER-EXPANDING MYSTERY

FISH USUALLY LIVE ONLY IN either fresh water or salt water. In fact, most fish die if you switch waters on them. So what were freshwater eels doing in the sea? And *where* exactly were they born at sea? The leptocephali the scientists had found were still pretty big—Grassi guessed they were at least a year old. So where were the babies? And where were the eggs? Too many questions! We need a map!

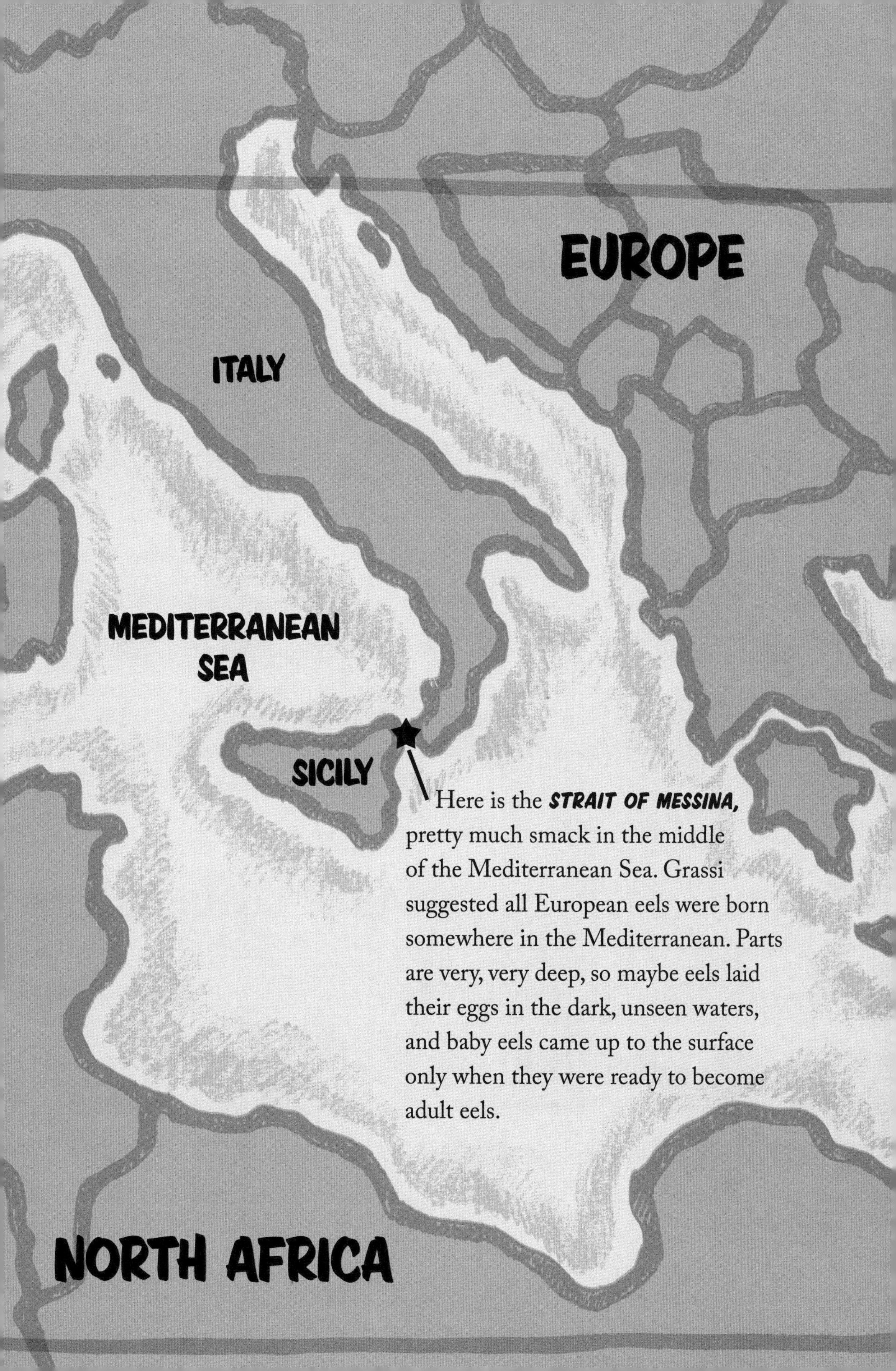

EUROPE

ITALY

MEDITERRANEAN
SEA

SICILY

NORTH AFRICA

Here is the **STRAIT OF MESSINA,**
pretty much smack in the middle
of the Mediterranean Sea. Grassi
suggested all European eels were born
somewhere in the Mediterranean. Parts
are very, very deep, so maybe eels laid
their eggs in the dark, unseen waters,
and baby eels came up to the surface
only when they were ready to become
adult eels.

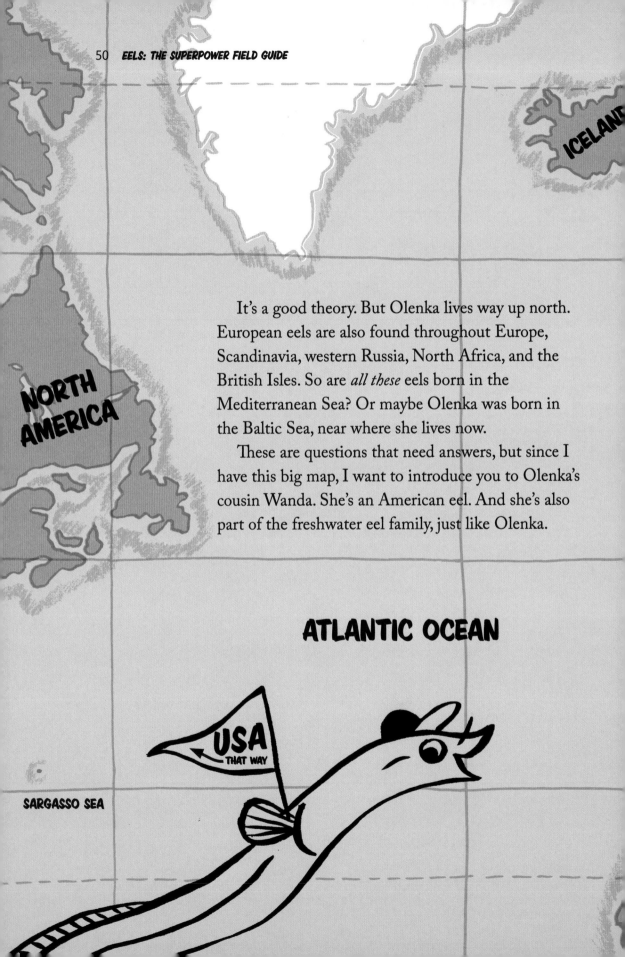

ICELAND

NORTH AMERICA

It's a good theory. But Olenka lives way up north. European eels are also found throughout Europe, Scandinavia, western Russia, North Africa, and the British Isles. So are *all these* eels born in the Mediterranean Sea? Or maybe Olenka was born in the Baltic Sea, near where she lives now.

These are questions that need answers, but since I have this big map, I want to introduce you to Olenka's cousin Wanda. She's an American eel. And she's also part of the freshwater eel family, just like Olenka.

ATLANTIC OCEAN

USA
THAT WAY

SARGASSO SEA

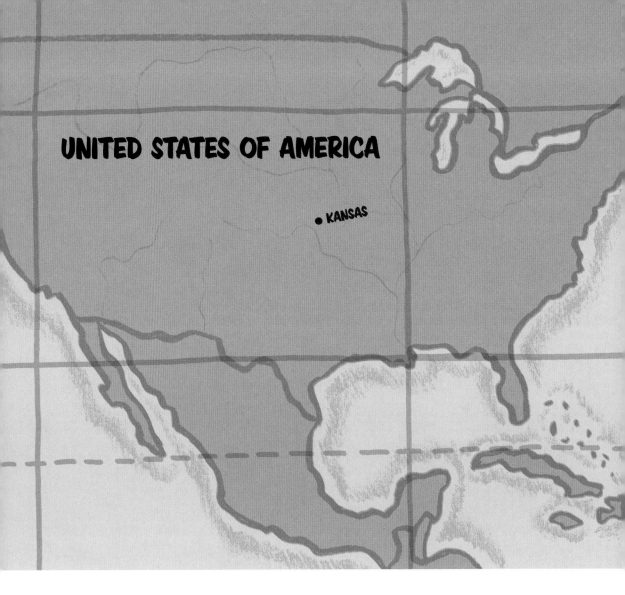

Wanda lives on the other side of the Atlantic Ocean in a little river in Kansas, in the middle of the United States of America. Kansas, as you might know, is where Dorothy and Toto lived before a tornado whisked them away to the Land of Oz.

Wanda looks exactly like Olenka. They're the same fishy-brown color. They both live in pleasantly muddy rivers. They both have **OXYGEN SKIN** and **SLIMETASTIC SAFETY SHIELDS**. In fact, if a tornado ever whisked Wanda over to Olenka's river, you would have a very hard time knowing who was who.

It might seem weird that two animals living on opposite sides of a great big ocean should look exactly alike, but it's actually not that weird. If you've read my book about beavers (which you should—Elmer is really great), you'll know that beavers on either side of the Atlantic Ocean look exactly the same too.

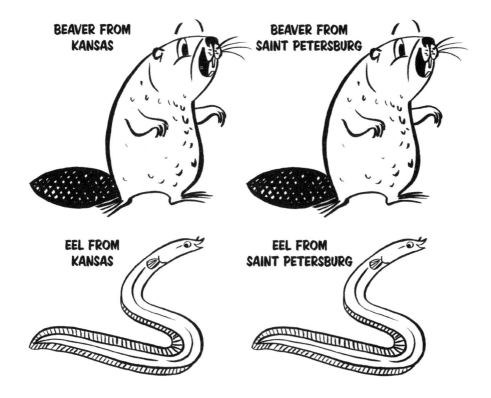

BEAVER FROM KANSAS

BEAVER FROM SAINT PETERSBURG

EEL FROM KANSAS

EEL FROM SAINT PETERSBURG

But do you know what would be really weird? If a North American beaver living in Kansas (where Wanda lives) and a Eurasian beaver living north of Saint Petersburg (where Olenka lives) were born in exactly the same place. Impossible! There is absolutely no way two animals living 5,000 miles (8,050 kilometers) apart could possibly have the same location on their birth certificate.

You know that. And I know that. But I'm not sure Olenka and Wanda know that.

So are you ready? Time to solve **THE GREAT EEL MYSTERY.**

THE DEEP BLUE VASTNESS

IT'S 1904. THE DANISH RESEARCH SHIP *Thor* is anchored near the Faroe Islands in the middle of the North Atlantic Ocean. There is a man aboard named Johannes Schmidt, and he has just found something in a fishing net. It looks like a see-through leaf-fish.

Now, Schmidt knew fish. He was part of a Danish team of marine biologists hired to study fish larvae, so he knew what he'd found: a baby European eel in the Atlantic Ocean. What was it doing out there? Was it lost? Had it been washed out of the Mediterranean on a giant tide? Schmidt didn't know, but he was going to find out.

Over the next few years, Schmidt sailed between Iceland and France, netting more eel larvae. They were all around three inches (7.5 centimeters) long, about the same size as the larvae Grassi had found in the Mediterranean. And that could mean only one thing: The answer to **THE GREAT EEL MYSTERY** wasn't in the Mediterranean Sea or anywhere close to European rivers. The answer lay somewhere in the middle of the Atlantic Ocean. Somewhere out there, in the deep blue vastness, European eels met, spawned, and laid their eggs. But where?

The Atlantic Ocean isn't just big. It's ridiculously big. It covers 20 percent of the earth's surface, or about 40 million square miles of water. And that's only the surface. Remember, oceans go deep, deep down, hundreds, sometimes thousands of feet. Scientists estimate that the

Atlantic has 80 million cubic miles (330 million cubic kilometers) of water. That sounds like a lot, but let me explain how much water that really is. Imagine a box a mile long by a mile high by a mile wide. (That's a big box!) Now imagine how much water it would take to fill that box. (A lot of water!) Now imagine how much water you'd need to fill *80 million* of those boxes (!). Now imagine trying to find a tiny, almost invisible baby eel somewhere in those 80 million boxes of dark blue seawater. (**DOUBLE INVISIBILITY** in overdrive!)

Sounds impossible, doesn't it? But Schmidt had found a clue to a fishy mystery thousands of years old, and he was going to solve it. Schmidt crisscrossed that vast ocean for years and years *and years,* dragging nets through those 80 million cubic miles of water. He caught thousands of baby eels. And eel by eel, Schmidt began to see a pattern. The farther south he sailed, and the farther west, the smaller and smaller the larvae became.

Schmidt had to take a break for World War I, and his second ship sank to the bottom of the sea. But one fine day in 1922, 3,500 miles (5,600 kilometers) from where he discovered his first baby eel and after *two long decades* of searching, Schmidt found himself in a mysterious part of the Atlantic Ocean called the Sargasso Sea.

Strange tales have been told about the Sargasso Sea for hundreds of years. It was said to be a place where abandoned ships would be found drifting with only skeletons aboard. Sailors told stories of sea monsters and of seaweed so thick, ships would be dragged down. And some of those stories are probably true.

You see, the Sargasso Sea is a large egg-shaped area in the middle-ish of the Atlantic Ocean, named for its thick mats of brown *sargassum* seaweed, which some sailors, including Christopher Columbus's crew, said were too thick to sail through. But what makes the Sargasso so strange and special are the powerful ocean currents flowing all around it. They flow in a giant fast-moving clockwise circle known as the North Atlantic Gyre, while in the middle, like the eye of a storm, the waters of the Sargasso Sea are oddly still, warm, and salty.

These ocean currents are what first carried European sailing ships to the Americas. Ships would sail south to catch the southwesterly currents off the coast of Africa. To get back to Europe, they sailed north with the Gulf Stream, up past Canada, then across. Unlucky sailors who tried to sail directly east or west through the breathless Sargasso Sea could be caught without winds for weeks, marooned at sea under a scorching sun.

It was here, in the Sargasso Sea, that Schmidt found a baby eel 0.4 inches long (10 millimeters) and probably only a few days old. Schmidt had finally cracked **THE GREAT EEL MYSTERY!** He'd discovered the **SUPERSECRET LAIR OF THE ABYSS**—sort of.

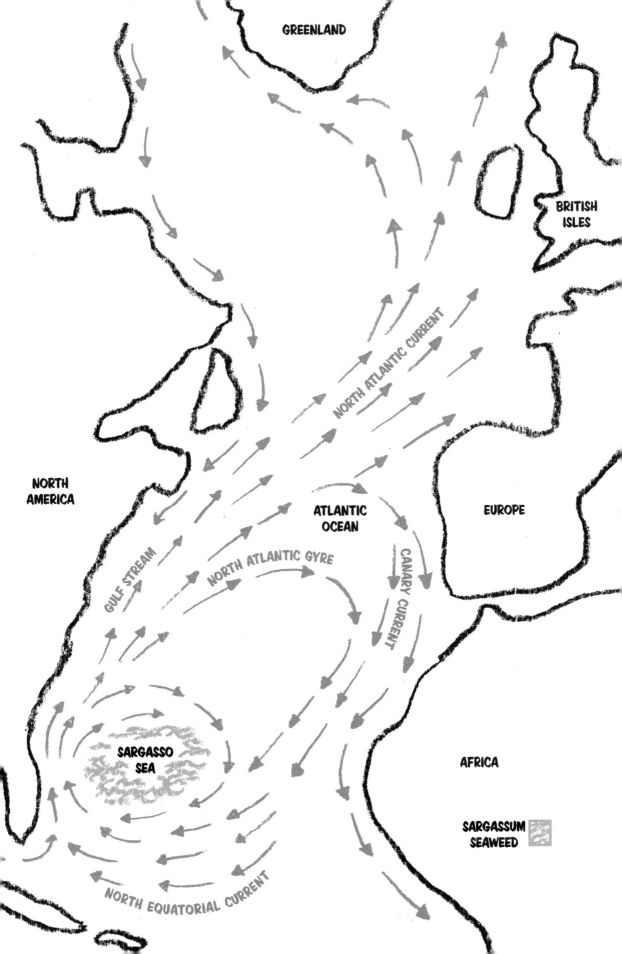

Sadly, the Sargasso Sea is becoming a giant garbage patch. Because ocean currents flow all around it—but not through it—trash collects in the calm waters and never gets washed out. Most of the garbage is made up of plastics, and most of those plastics have been broken down by waves and sunlight into millions and millions of tiny pieces. Those tiny pieces swirl around in the ocean, like a terrible peppery soup that can harm or kill any birds, fish, or marine life that eat them.

SUPERPOWER #6

SUPERSECRET LAIR OF THE ABYSS

BATMAN HAS HIS BATCAVE. Superman has his Fortress of Solitude. And European eels have their **SUPERSECRET LAIR OF THE ABYSS.** (As you might know, "lair" is a fancy word for a hideout, and "abyss" means the very deepest, darkest depths.)

Can a hideout be a superpower? I say it can when it's so well hidden, so extraordinarily, fantastically, impossibly secret, no one has *ever* found the entrance. Even Superman can't say that about his Fortress of Solitude.

Scientists have made eels produce eggs by giving them hormones, but no scientist, despite endless searching, has ever seen European eels spawn naturally.

You see, Schmidt had found the general area where eels are born, but no one—not Schmidt, nor any scientist since—has ever tracked an adult eel from Europe all the way back to the Sargasso Sea. No one has ever seen European eels spawn—and believe me, they've tried! Scientists just presume this is where it happens because they've found newly hatched leptocephali here and nowhere else. That's what I call a **SUPERSECRET LAIR OF THE ABYSS!**

The Sargasso Sea is only a small part of the Atlantic, but it is still enormous. It covers about two million square miles (5,200,000 square kilometers) of water, and parts of it are more than four miles (7,000 meters) deep. Do you remember the boxes of seawater—a mile wide by a mile high by a mile deep? Well, the Sargasso has about eight million of those boxes. Somewhere in there, in the complete darkness, at the bottom of this mysterious abyss, European eels are born.

Have you ever heard of the Bermuda Triangle? If you draw lines connecting Florida, Bermuda, and Puerto Rico, the area in the middle is famous for being weird—a place where ships and planes supposedly just *disappear*. And wouldn't you know, the Sargasso Sea covers part of the Bermuda Triangle. Mystery upon mystery.

And do you remember Wanda from Kansas? Weirdly enough, Wanda was born here too. Olenka's family from Europe and Wanda's family from North America—eels that spend their lives thousands and thousands of miles apart—all come together and spawn in the dark depths of the mysterious Sargasso Sea. (They don't spawn exactly in the same place. European eels are a little to the east.) These mysterious animals swim for months across the vast blue ocean. They somehow find the right spot, come together, spawn, and die. And to this day, no one has ever seen them do it. Never. Ever. And that's why it's **THE GREAT EEL MYSTERY.**

Okay. **LET'S PUT ALL YOUR KNOWLEDGE TO THE TEST!**

QUIZ #2

CAN YOU FIND OLENKA AND WANDA?

WARNING: These two are super sneaky! (Answers are on p.94.)

SUPERPOWER #7

GLOBE-SPANNING GRIT

CAN WE DEDICATE THIS CHAPTER to Johannes Schmidt? Because if anyone has ever had **GLOBE-SPANNING GRIT,** it's Schmidt. Hats off to Schmidt!

Johannes Schmidt
1877 – 1933

Now back to Olenka.

Let's review what we know. When Olenka was just a tiny, transparent, leaf-shaped baby, she traveled from the abyss of the Sargasso Sea all the way to the Baltic Sea. That's more than 3,700 miles (6,000 kilometers)! ***ABSOLUTELY ASTONISHING!*** When anyone—fish, bird, man, woman, bug, or butterfly—does anything this gobsmackingly impressive, I have to ask two big questions: How do they do it? And why? Let's start with the how.

HOW DO THEY SWIM SO FAR?

No one really knows. Scientists think they catch the Gulf Stream north from the Sargasso, which carries them on the northeasterly current to Europe.

HOW LONG DOES IT TAKE?

No one really knows. Probably somewhere between nine months and three years. Scientists have dropped bottles in the ocean to see how fast the currents carry them to Europe.

WHAT DO THEY EAT?

Nobody really knows. Probably marine snow. It looks like tiny snowflakes falling through the deep ocean, but it's actually specks of dead animals, skin flakes, and gross stuff like that. However, baby eels have daggerlike teeth. If they eat marine snow, why do they need dagger teeth? Nobody really knows.

AND NOW FOR THE WHY.

Scientists think European eels have been doing this crazy journey for 50 million years. Back then, the Atlantic Ocean was much smaller. You see, between the Sargasso Sea and Europe is something called the Mid-Atlantic Ridge—it's a crack that runs right down the middle of the Atlantic along the ocean floor. Scientists call it a **spreading ridge,** which means lava is constantly bubbling up through that crack. As the lava cools, it makes new ocean floor, which pushes the sides of the crack farther and farther apart. And that means the Atlantic Ocean is forever getting bigger. Only a little each year, but over 50 million years, the Atlantic Ocean has grown huge, which means eels are traveling farther and farther and farther.

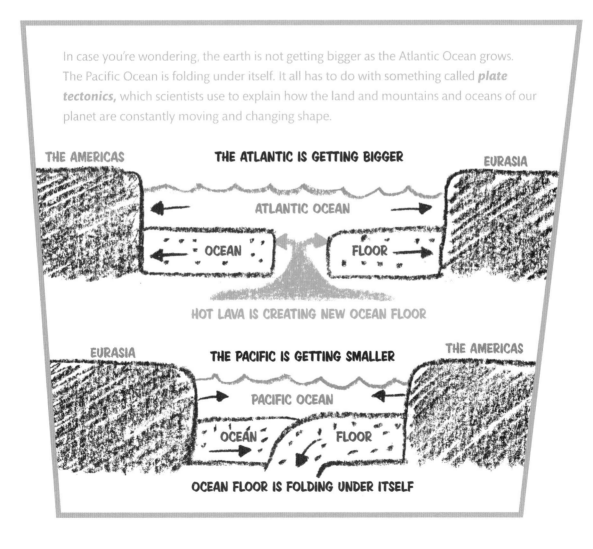

In case you're wondering, the earth is not getting bigger as the Atlantic Ocean grows. The Pacific Ocean is folding under itself. It all has to do with something called **plate tectonics,** which scientists use to explain how the land and mountains and oceans of our planet are constantly moving and changing shape.

THE AMERICAS   **THE ATLANTIC IS GETTING BIGGER**   EURASIA

ATLANTIC OCEAN

OCEAN   FLOOR

HOT LAVA IS CREATING NEW OCEAN FLOOR

EURASIA   **THE PACIFIC IS GETTING SMALLER**   THE AMERICAS

PACIFIC OCEAN

OCEAN   FLOOR

OCEAN FLOOR IS FOLDING UNDER ITSELF

*NOT TO SCALE

SALTWATER

EGG: Males and females spawn, perhaps together in a large group, somewhere in the abyss of the Sargasso Sea. Scientists think females lay between 10 and 20 million eggs.

LIFE

SILVER EEL: Mature eels travel downstream and undergo one final metamorphosis as they begin their journey back to the Sargasso Sea. It is only while at sea, in the deep, dark unknown, that silver eels will develop eggs and milt (or sperm), ready for spawning.

FRESHWATER

YELLOW EEL: Adult eels live quietly for five to twenty years or more. An eel in Sweden lived to be 155 years old! In 1859, an eight-year-old boy threw it into a well, and there it lived until 2014. Size: Females can reach four feet (1.2 meters). Males are usually shorter.

LEPTOCEPHALUS: Flat and transparent, baby eels drift with ocean currents toward Europe for a year or more. As they approach the coastline, they slowly shape-shift into glass eels. Size: 0.4–3.0 inches (10–75 millimeters). Yes, you're seeing right: Leptocephali are fatter and longer than the glass eels they shape-shift into.

CYCLE

GLASS EEL: Every spring, glass eels come wiggling and tumbling into the mouths of rivers around Europe and the Mediterranean. They are eel-shaped with fins. As they begin to eat normal eel food like bugs and such, they slowly gain color. Size: 2.0–3.0 inches (50–75 millimeters).

ELVER: Scientists think males stay in the **estuaries,** where the ocean and rivers meet, while only the females travel upstream to find their perfect spot. In fact, scientists believe eels only fully become male or female when they reach fresh water. Size: 3.0–4.0 inches (75–100 millimeters).

HOME SWEET HOME

IT'S A COLD, DARK AUTUMN NIGHT. There's a new moon—barely a sliver of light in the dark sky. Something is happening, but with my mere human senses, I don't have a clue what it is. Maybe it's the darkness. Maybe there's a particular wind or smell in the air. Maybe hundreds of miles away, the tides have turned. But *something* is starting . . .

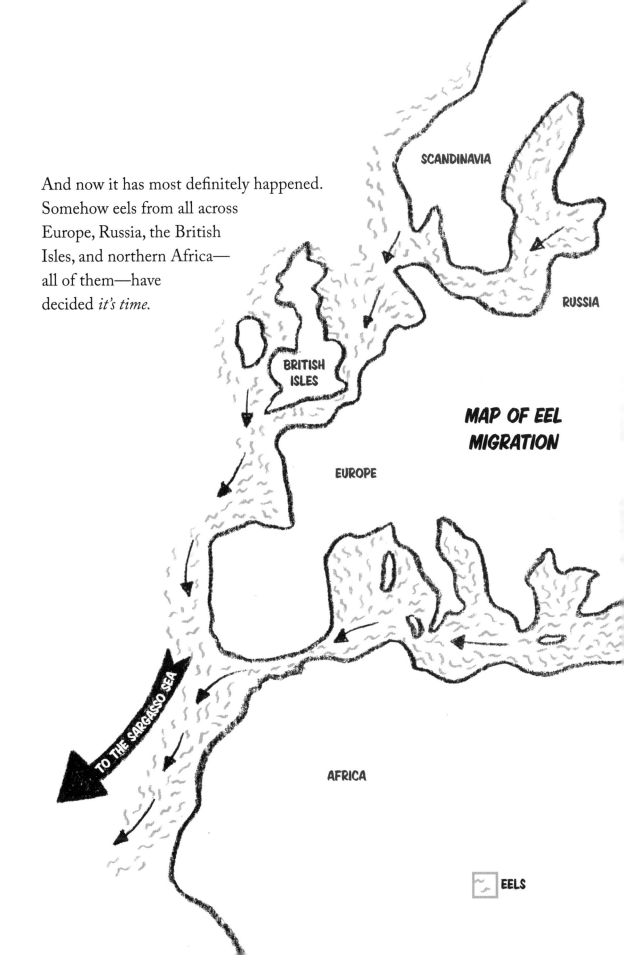

And now it has most definitely happened. Somehow eels from all across Europe, Russia, the British Isles, and northern Africa— all of them—have decided *it's time*.

SCANDINAVIA

RUSSIA

BRITISH
ISLES

MAP OF EEL
MIGRATION

EUROPE

TO THE SARGASSO SEA

AFRICA

EELS

How? Nobody really knows. For eighteen years, Olenka has led a lonely life, but now she acts as part of a mysterious group.

I know I've only just explained how Olenka arrived at her river, but it's time for her to return to her first home, her birthplace, the Sargasso Sea. Before she can begin, she must shape-shift one last time into an **OCEAN-STEALTH SUBMARINE.**

SUPERPOWER #8

OCEAN-STEALTH SUBMARINE MODE

OLENKA FOLLOWS THE RIVER DOWNSTREAM, mile after mile. As she travels, she eats. A lot. She devours little fish. She gobbles up bugs and snails like gumdrops. She guzzles and gulps, binges and gorges, and grows fatter and fatter and fatter. By the time she reaches the sea, Olenka will have more than 25 percent body fat.

The fat is fuel for her trip back to the Sargasso. But Olenka needs more than fuel—she needs to become a whole new fish. Riverboats don't try to cross a vast open ocean, and the same goes for river fish. Time to activate **OCEAN-STEALTH SUBMARINE MODE!**

Ocean waters can be dark. Olenka needs deep-sea goggles. Her eyes grow 50 percent larger and turn from a purplish color to yellow. Yellow eyes are much better for deep-sea looking.

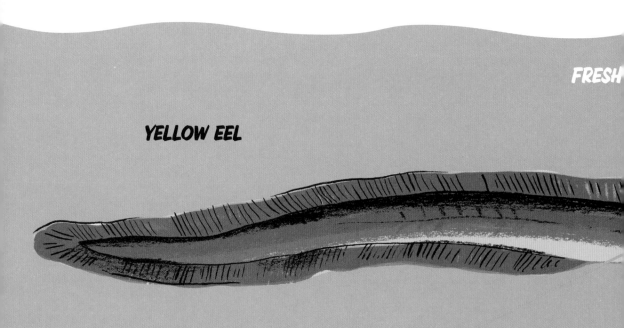

FRESH

YELLOW EEL

YELLOW BELLY

Ocean waters are full of predators. A brownish-yellowish-greenish body is good camouflage in a muddy river, but not in the open sea. Olenka's belly turns white and her back silver, the better to blend in with the sparkling ocean waters.

Ocean waters are deep and fast-moving. Her pectoral fins grow larger (although—let's be honest—those fins are still pretty small to cross an ocean), and various changes happen to her organs, muscles, and gills to help her swim and keep afloat in the open sea.

And finally, ocean waters are salty. Olenka is a freshwater fish, and most freshwater fish die if you put them in salt water. Why? It has to do with how fish balance the water and salts inside their bodies with the saltiness of the water around them, or what scientists call *osmoregulation*. It's a bit complicated, but think of it like this:

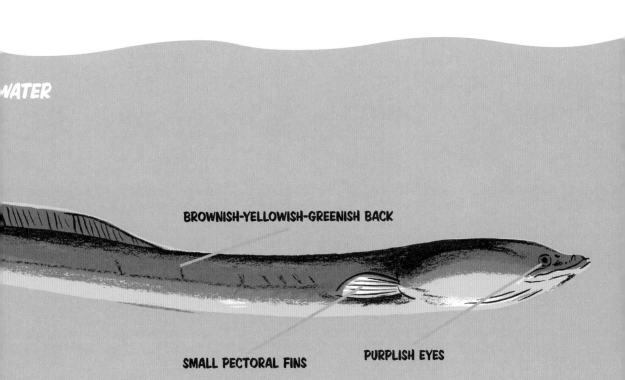

WATER

BROWNISH-YELLOWISH-GREENISH BACK

SMALL PECTORAL FINS

PURPLISH EYES

You probably know seawater is far too salty for you to drink. Now imagine a freshwater fish plunked into the saltiest seawater—way too much salt! Of course, ocean fish are built to handle the salt, but a freshwater fish isn't. In fact, if a freshwater fish suddenly found itself in water that was much saltier than its own body, the fish would lose water until it dies of dehydration. Terrible! (In case you're interested, most seawater fish can't handle fresh water either.)

It might take a couple of weeks for Olenka to adjust to a salty world, and while her body changes, her **SLIMETASTIC SAFETY SHIELD** helps her survive without too much trauma.

And finally, weirdest of all, her stomach and guts begin to shrink and shrivel. Once Olenka is at sea, she will *never eat again*. The whole way

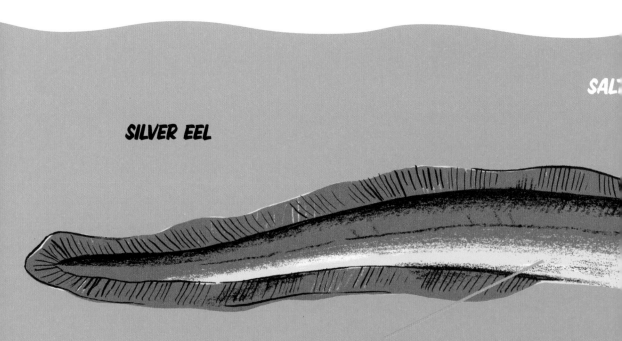

SAL

SILVER EEL

WHITE BELLY

across the Atlantic Ocean, which maybe takes six or nine months or maybe even longer, she doesn't eat a single bite. And scientists have no idea why.

But for now, Olenka has reached the Baltic Sea. She is very fat. And that leads us into some dark waters.

Most superheroes have a weakness. Superman can't stand Kryptonite. Wonder Woman weakens if she's chained. Eels have a weakness too. Actually, it's more of a super weakness, and it is about to kill off eels completely. I'm sorry to say this, but European eels are on the brink of extinction.

Fish that are able to go between fresh and salt water are called **euryhaline** fish. Another euryhaline fish is the salmon, which spends its life at sea but breeds in freshwater rivers—the exact opposite of Olenka.

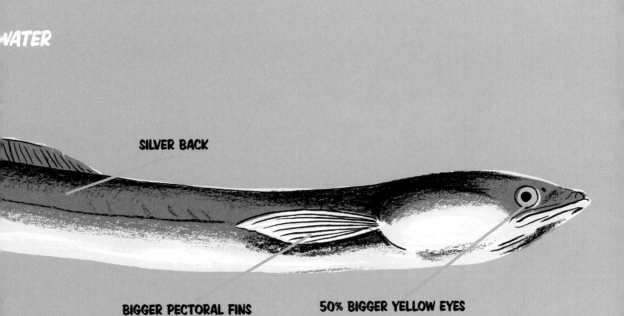

WATER

SILVER BACK

BIGGER PECTORAL FINS   50% BIGGER YELLOW EYES

SUPER WEAKNESS: SUPER DELICIOUSNESS

EELS USED TO BE one of the most common fish in European rivers. Not anymore. European eels are now critically endangered—that's one step away from being extinct. And it has happened very suddenly. Since the 1980s, European eel populations have fallen by as much as 99 percent. Imagine a hundred dogs running around a park. Then only one. Shocking! Horrifying! People would want to know why. And scientists definitely have theories about why eels are disappearing.

Some scientists say the ocean currents are changing. River pollution and parasites are also a problem. Dams are blocking the eels' migration upriver and killing the eels as they try to come back down. All of these are very big and terrible problems. But some say these are nothing compared to one very simple problem: Too many people are eating too many eels.

You see, freshwater eels are delicious. The fatter they get, the more delicious they become, and mature European eels, American eels, and Japanese eels are considered the most scrumptious of all. Smoked eels, jellied eels, fried eels, eel pie, eels stewed in almond milk, eels grilled with salty sauce. For as long as humans have known how to catch and cook fish, they have eaten eels.

The Japanese might like eel more than anyone in the world. They eat about 70 percent of all the eels caught worldwide, or more than 100,000 tons of eels each year. They particularly like smoked eel—it's called *unagi*. Eating *unagi* is part of a traditional Japanese summer festival, sort of like how some Americans eat turkey at Christmas.

Japanese eels, European eels, and American eels are all almost exactly the same. So when Japanese eels started to disappear, *unagi* lovers looked to Europe. (Apparently American eels aren't quite as tasty.) Merchants pay European fishermen to catch glass eels as they come wiggling and tumbling into rivers each spring. The little eels are flown to Asia and raised in tanks until they grow into yellow eels. Then they are cooked, smoked, and sold to restaurants all over the world.

But European eel populations were also dwindling. In 2010, the European Union banned exports of European eels. That was good, except that a black market sprang up, first in Europe and then in North America. A black market is when things are bought and sold that shouldn't be—like stolen paintings and rhinoceros horns. Eel dealers have paid fishermen up to two thousand dollars a pound for glass eels. It's totally illegal, but that doesn't stop anyone.

Do you know the worst part about all this? The worst part is that no one even knows eels are critically endangered, and very few people seem to care. Maybe it's because eels aren't cute and cuddly like pandas. Or maybe it's because they're so tasty that no one wants to stop eating them. But now you know. And hopefully you care.

Japanese scientists have worked to raise eels in fish farms for decades, and they still haven't succeeded. Japanese eels have the same wondrously mysterious life cycle as Olenka—in fact, their birthplace, near the Mariana Islands, some 185 miles (300 kilometers) away from Japan, wasn't discovered until 1991.

It's time for your last quiz, but we need to keep moving. I want Olenka to get to the Atlantic Ocean as fast as possible. How about I just tell you a weird eel fact instead?

WEIRD EEL FACT: DEADLY BLOOD

EEL BLOOD IS TOXIC TO MAMMALS. It's downright deadly for humans, but that doesn't stop us from eating eels. The toxins disappear when eels are cooked, which is why eels are never eaten raw. In fact, eel blood is so toxic, it won the Nobel Prize. I'm not joking.

You see, a century ago, a French scientist named Charles Richet was interested in immunization. As you might know, immunization gives people a tiny bit of a disease so their bodies are able to fight off the whole, full-blown disease. In his various tests and trials, Richet experimented with toxic eel blood and identified the deadly allergic reaction now known as anaphylaxis. (Peanuts and bee stings can give some people this sort of allergic reaction.) Richet won the Nobel Prize for Medicine in 1913. And he couldn't have done it without European eels.

1913

SUPERPOWER #9

FOUR-NOSTRILED NAVIGATION

OLENKA HAS SLIPPED PAST THE FISHERMEN. She's escaped
every danger that awaited her. She has fully shape-shifted into a silver
eel and is ready to set sail. But how do eels know where to go? How do
you begin a 3,700-mile (6,000-kilometer) journey across a vast blue sea
without a single signpost?

Would you believe she smells her way there?

Maybe you've heard that sharks can smell blood in the ocean from
miles away. Scientists say they can smell one drop among 10 billion
drops of water; that's one drop of blood in an Olympic-size swimming
pool. Impressive, right? Well, scientists say eels can detect one speck of
their favorite worms sprinkled through *10 trillion drops* of water. That's
like one pinch of worm in 1,000 swimming pools. Never underestimate
Olenka's nose.

ONE DROP
IN TEN
BILLION

ONE SPECK
IN TEN
TRILLION
DROPS

For starters, she has four nostrils! Actually, most fish have four
nostrils, but most fish can't smell the saltiness of a particular tide.
Olenka can. And if you had taken Olenka from her river and carried her
over hills and valleys and far away, she would have found her way home
to her river. Baby eels can probably smell fresh water while they're at sea

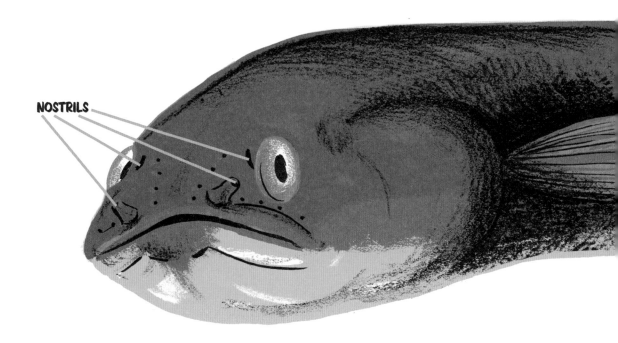

NOSTRILS

and point themselves toward a river. For all I know, Olenka can smell the Sargasso Sea from the Baltic. I'm not saying she can. But I'm not saying she can't.

And here is something else scientists don't understand. All European eels breed together in the same place, which means there is no biological difference between eels from Morocco or Russia or Ireland or Turkey. So why do some young eels swim to Russia and others to Turkey? Why do some eels urge themselves upstream for hundreds of miles? Will Olenka's daughters find their way up to her river? Can children navigate by a smell they've never smelled? Nobody knows.

But we do know that animals have senses we can never begin to understand—like the smell map in Olenka's brain. Perhaps she's using it right now to find her way through the Baltic Sea and south toward the Azores. From there she'll catch the Canary Current westward. But she doesn't do it by smell alone. Olenka has one last superpower making sure she is always on the right path.

SUPERPOWER #10

THE MAGNETIC HEAD

HAVE YOU EVER BEEN DRIVING with your family in a new city, and your parents take out a map? Or maybe they look at a map on their phone, and a little dot shows them *exactly* where they are. As your

parents drive, that little dot will keep moving, always showing them where they are and where they need to go. Human technology is amazing. But European eels have been doing the same thing for *millions of years,* and they don't need a phone or a blinking dot. Eels have the extraordinary biological power of **THE MAGNETIC HEAD!**

And I really do mean Olenka has magnets in her head. Eels have tiny crystals of iron in their heads that they use to guide themselves along the

magnetic paths of the world. It's like having a world globe inside your brain so you always know exactly where you are.

Scientists call it *magnetoreception.* They think long-distant travelers like homing pigeons, salmon, and sea turtles have iron crystals in their heads or beaks to help them navigate.

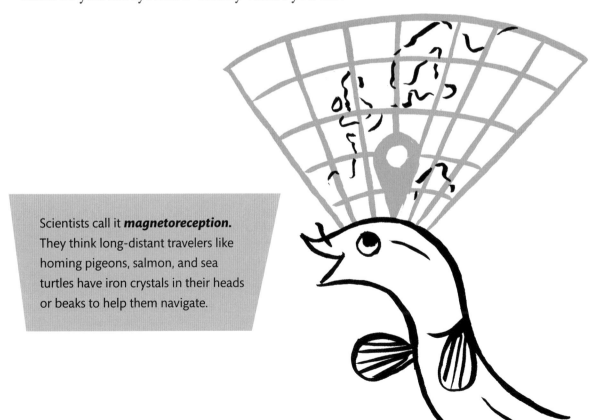

THE MAGNETIC HEAD works much more like a map than a compass. A compass will point you in the right direction, but it doesn't tell you the easiest route or what obstacles might be in your way. Scientists have discovered that baby eels don't point themselves directly northeast toward Europe—which is what a compass would tell them to do. Instead, **THE MAGNETIC HEAD** tells them to go northwest, what looks like the wrong direction. But by swimming northwest, young eels can catch the Gulf Stream, which will carry them far more swiftly to the coast of Europe.

It's pretty funny when you think about. Here is an animal that no one has been able to track, and yet it has a built-in world map and always knows exactly where it is. And this animal with a sophisticated geo-locating tool in her head just spent eighteen years in the very same spot of the very same river. Olenka is a mystery. No doubt about it.

While we were talking, Olenka slipped out to sea. She is gone forever into the deep blue vastness. I hope she makes it all the way home.

INTRODUCING OLENKA:

MIGRATING MISTRESS OF MYSTERY!

IF I HAD TOLD YOU at the beginning that this book was about a creature with four nostrils and magnets in her head, who shape-shifts from a leaf to a noodle to a snake, who climbs 100-foot walls without hands and breathes through jelly-coated skin just as easily on land as underwater, who somehow travels for thousands and thousands of miles without eating a single bite and without anyone ever tracking her journey, and who has kept her birthplace so secret no one has ever found her eggs, what would you have said?

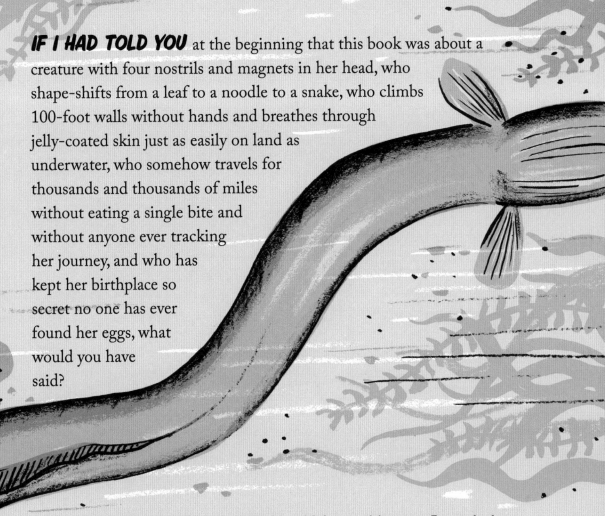

I would have said such an animal couldn't possibly exist. It might be an alien or a dream creature, but definitely not a plain and homely eel.

Olenka is not pretty or majestic. She doesn't have luxurious fur or beautiful feathers. She is plain, brown, slimy . . . and wildly, absolutely, mystifyingly extraordinary. Olenka is one of a kind. She is a true Humble Hero.

I don't think any animal can top the mysterious wonders of the European eel. But creatures all have their own unique sets of superpowers that make each and every one extraordinary in its own special way. Wait until you hear about **BARNABUS THE WARTHOG, TWOMBLY THE TERMITE,** and **PEPPER THE LEAST WEASEL** . . .

GLOSSARY

AMPHIBIAN (am-FIB-bee-an): a group of vertebrates including frogs, newts, and salamanders. They need a moist or watery environment to survive and can breathe through their skin.

ANAL FIN (AY-nal fin): the fin on the underside of a fish, near its bum.

CAUDAL FIN (CAW-dal fin): a fancy way of saying "fish tail."

CAVIAR (CAH-vee-are): the eggs of sturgeon, eaten as a dainty delicacy.

CUTANEOUS RESPIRATION (cue-TAY-knee-us res-pee-RAY-shun): breathing through your skin.

DORSAL FIN (DOOR-sal fin): the fin along a fish's back. Great white sharks probably have the most famous dorsal fins.

ELVERS: young eels.

ESTUARIES (ESS-chew-air-rees): the mouths of rivers where they meet the sea. The water is somewhat salty, not quite fresh but not properly salty like seawater.

EURYHALINE (your-ee-HAY-line): a creature that can survive in fresh or salty water.

FRESHWATER EELS: a special group of eels that are born at sea but spend their adult lives in fresh water. There are nineteen species, including European eels (like Olenka), North American eels, and Japanese eels.

GILLS: organs for breathing underwater.

GILL FILAMENTS (gill FILL-a-ments): the pink, feathery parts inside gills that absorb oxygen from the water.

GLASS EELS: young eels that do not yet have color. They look like thin glass noodles.

LARVAE (LAR-vay): the young or immature forms of a creature.

LEPTOCEPHALUS (LEP-toe-SEF-a-lus): transparent, leaf-shaped baby eels.

MAGNETORECEPTION (magnet-o-re-SEP-shun): the ability to sense and navigate by the earth's magnetic field.

METAMORPHOSIS (met-a-MOR-foe-sis): a complete change, like how a tadpole changes into a frog or how a frog can become a handsome prince in fairy tales.

OSMOREGULATION (OZ-mo-reg-you-LAY-shun): balancing the water and salts in a body.

OXYGEN (OX-ee-jen): You can't see it, but it's all around you, and you need to breathe it to survive.

PARASITES (PAIR-a-sites): pests that live on or inside another living thing and usually make it unhappy and unhealthy.

PECTORAL FINS (PECK-tore-al fins): the fins on either side of a fish's face.

PLATE TECTONICS (plate teck-TON-ics): the theory that the earth's outer layer is made of large pieces called plates that are constantly moving and shifting over a wobbly layer of liquid lava.

SARGASSUM (sar-GAS-some): brown seaweed that floats in large, island-like clumps.

SPREADING RIDGE: a crack through the earth's crust through which lava bubbles up to create new crust.

SURFACE TENSION: a holding-together or tightness across the surface of a liquid. It lets tiny creatures float and slide on water.

VERTEBRAE (VERT-uh-bray): the bones in an animal's spine. They form a line from the base of the skull to the tailbone.

ANSWERS TO QUIZ #2

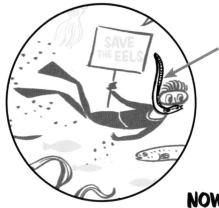

OLENKA is pretending to be a snorkel and **WANDA** is hiding among the octopus's arms.

NOW *THAT'S* SNEAKY!

FURTHER EEL READING

IF YOU WANT TO KNOW MORE about the mysterious life of eels, you might enjoy the books below. **WARNING:** They are written for adults. But that doesn't mean they are not interesting.

Eels: An Exploration, from New Zealand to the Sargasso, of the World's Most Mysterious Fish by James Prosek (Harper, 2010)

The Book of Eels by Tom Fort (HarperCollins, 2002)

AND HERE ARE SOME WONDERFUL VIDEOS AND IMAGES TO CHECK OUT

A SUITCASE FULL OF EELS: A wonderful collection of eel-inspired art by students in the Illustration degree program at the University of Plymouth, in England: eels.cargocollective.com/ILLUS510

ELI THE EEL: A MYSTERIOUS MIGRATION: A TED-Ed Animation Lesson by James Prosek: ed.ted.com/lessons/eli-the-eel-a-mysterious-migration-james-prosek#watch

NATURE'S HUMBLE HEROES!
AVAILABLE AT A BOOKSTORE
NEAR YOU!!